LANCASTER PAMPHLETS

The Counter-Reformation

and the Catholic Reformation
in early modern Europe

Michael Mullett

METHUEN · LONDON AND NEW YORK

First published in 1984 by
Methuen & Co. Ltd
11 New Fetter Lane,
London EC4P 4EE

Published in the USA by
Methuen & Co.
in association with Methuen, Inc.
733 Third Avenue, New York,
NY 10017

British Library Cataloguing in
Publication Data

Mullett, Michael A.
The Counter-Reformation and
the Catholic Reformation
in early modern Europe.
– (Lancaster pamphlets)
1. Counter-Reformation
I. Title   II. Series
270.6   BR430

ISBN 0–416–36060–2

© 1984 Michael Mullett

Typeset in Great Britain by
Scarborough Typesetting Services
and printed by
Richard Clay (The Chaucer Press)
Bungay, Suffolk

Contents

Foreword vii

Introduction: new views of the Counter-Reformation 1

The origins of the Counter-Reformation 5

The stirrings of Catholic reform 11

The priesthood 15

The Society of Jesus and other orders 22

The popular impact of the Counter-Reformation 26

Success and failure in the Counter-Reformation 30

The politics of the Counter-Reformation 32

Missions 37

Conclusion 44

Select bibliography 46

Foreword

Lancaster Pamphlets offer concise and up-to-date accounts of major historical topics, primarily for the help of students preparing for Advanced Level examinations, though they should also be of value to those pursuing introductory courses in universities and other institutions of higher education. They do not rely on prior textbook knowledge. Without being all-embracing, their aims are to bring some of the central themes or problems confronting students and teachers into sharper focus than the textbook writer can hope to do; to provide the reader with some of the results of recent research which the textbook may not embody; and to stimulate thought about the whole interpretation of the topic under discussion.

The Counter-Reformation
and the Catholic Reformation
in early modern Europe

Introduction: new views of the Counter-Reformation

Most traditional writing on the Counter-Reformation has accepted assumptions which will be questioned in this pamphlet. Historians used to assume that the Counter-Reformation originated at about the same time as the Protestant Reformation – that is to say, around 1517, when the German Protestant Reformer Martin Luther began his break with the Roman Catholic Church – and that it ended between about 1600 and 1650. Another aspect of that older approach was to stress the role in the Counter-Reformation of the following factors: a series of reforming popes; the Council of Trent; the Jesuits; the Inquisition and the Index of prohibited books. The last few years, however, have witnessed the emergence of a different way of looking at the Counter-Reformation. It is the purpose of this pamphlet to provide an introduction to this new approach.

The traditional themes can be seen in some short passages from well-used works (which have been chosen as illustrations, not in order to denigrate them). V. H. H. Green's *Renaissance and Reformation*, for instance, dates the beginning of the Counter-Reformation to the same time as the start of Luther's Protestant movement: 'If we are to trace the Counter-Reformation to an original source, we need to turn to the so-called Oratory of Divine

1

Love . . . established about 1517'. Green, in common with other historians of the older school of thought, also laid great stress on the foundation of the Jesuits: 'it was in this way that the Counter-Reformation received its greatest impetus.' The Jesuits were singled out because of their impact on the upper classes: they were 'confessors to kings and princes', and their colleges catered for 'those who were to take their place in the world as men of power and position'.

A specialist historian of the Counter-Reformation, H. O. Evennett, shared the tendency to see the process as taking place over a short period of time: 'It was in active movement from the early decades of the sixteenth century to the middle decades of the seventeenth.' More recently, A. G. Dickens also wrote as if the Counter-Reformation was over relatively quickly: 'We have here considered the Counter-Reformation, properly so called, to have terminated around the middle of the seventeenth century.' An even shorter time-scale appeared in B. J. Kidd's well-used account: the Counter-Reformation 'reached its limit about the end of the [sixteenth] century'. In common with most writers in the 'traditional' school, Kidd thought that the Counter-Reformation started within the sixteenth century 'from a revival of religion discernible first in the Oratory of Divine Love'. Also, in line with the earlier thought on the Counter-Reformation, Kidd concentrated on the contribution of powerful, centralized institutions; these 'instruments' included in particular the Inquisition ('set to work by the papacy') and the Council of Trent.

This pamphlet takes a different approach. First, the origins of the Counter-Reformation are traced back beyond the sixteenth century into the middle ages. Second, the Counter-Reformation is viewed as a long-range process which was certainly not accomplished by 1600 or 1650. The vitality of the Counter-Reformation survived the end of a line of important reforming popes. The Council of Trent was indispensable to the Counter-Reformation, even though most people could never understand its lengthy resolutions on doctrine; but its legislation had to be implemented, which took a long time, sometimes well over a century, in the various parts of Catholic Europe. If the Council does not receive separate treatment (though it is not ignored) in this pamphlet,

2

I have the precedent of H. O. Evennett (earlier mentioned as a 'traditionalist' historian of the Counter-Reformation); in writing the introduction to Evennett's *Spirit of the Counter-Reformation*, his editor, John Bossy, remarked that 'Evennett found it possible to construct a convincing and at least reasonably comprehensive plan of the Counter-Reformation almost without mentioning the Council of Trent'. Bossy added that Evennett was not completely convinced 'that a whole epoch of the Church had been fashioned by this Council, and events seem to have justified his caution.'

As to other aspects of the Counter-Reformation which have received extensive treatment in most textbooks, the Index of prohibited books should certainly not be made too much of; it was composed, often maladroitly, by intellectual censors and consisted in large part of titles which the majority of European Catholics could not or would not have read. Another favourite traditional Counter-Reformation sub-topic, the Inquisition, need not receive too much attention; its authority was admittedly fearsome in Spanish and papal dominions, but it was at best a negative instrument of the Counter-Reformation.

Each of the above factors played its part in the Counter-Reformation. But to understand what was really going on, it is necessary to take a broader view of the process, one that emphasizes the efforts of countless bishops, priests and members of religious orders and the impact of change on the 'peoples of Catholic Europe'. That last phrase is taken from a writer who is typical of the new approach to the Counter-Reformation, John Bossy. What Bossy does is to look at the impact of the Counter Reformation on the populace at large. Of course he considers institutions, especially the Council of Trent, but he is more concerned with the regions of Catholic Europe than with Rome or Trent. The following quotation from Bossy demonstrates the groups and factors which for him are self-evidently important in the Counter-Reformation: 'To the ordinary population . . . what the Counter-Reformation really meant was the institution amongst them by bishops empowered by the Council of Trent to enforce [a system of parochial conformity]. . . . The faithful Catholic was to attend Mass . . ., he was to receive the church's sacraments . . . from the hands of his parish priest who would baptize him, marry him, give him extreme unction on his deathbed, and bury him . . . the priest would hear and absolve his sins in the sacrament of penance.' Bossy takes for granted that the key human elements in a study of the Counter-Reformation are 'the ordinary population', 'the faithful Catholic', the local bishop, and, above all, the parish priest.

Bossy's approach closely resembles that of the French historian, Jean Delumeau, in *Catholicism between Luther and Voltaire*, except that Delumeau is even more insistent that we must take a slow, long-range view of the Counter-Reformation, seeing it operate gradually on the religious and social history of Catholic Europe. Whereas Kidd, for instance, brought the Counter-Reformation to a close in 1600, Delumeau demonstrates that over much of Europe the process had hardly started by the time of Kidd's 'final' date. 'The imposition of artificial periods', Delumeau writes, 'has deformed the history of the Counter-Reformation and obscured its chronological dimensions. In fact the Catholic religious renaissance stretched over several centuries. We have shown already that it started with a long preparatory period of concern and effort; then, once the Council [of Trent] was over, it was slow to infiltrate customs, institutions and hearts. [In France] the full effects of the religious revival . . . began to be felt only in the second half of the seventeenth and at the beginning of the eighteenth centuries.' Delumeau's interpretation is sharply different from the traditional timetable. Yet the evidence to support his outlook is overwhelming; to take but one telling example, no seminary (a priests' training college, crucial to the success of the Counter-Reformation) was set up in the key diocese of Paris until 1696, 133 years after the Council of Trent had required the establishment of such institutions in dioceses. (The Paris authorities might, of course, have excused themselves by claiming that with a university in the diocese they were observing the letter of Trent's legislation.)

In common with other recent historians of early modern Europe, Delumeau is aware of how long it took in that period to implement change and put well-meaning reforms into actual effect: corrupt and immovable vested interests resisted improvements; administrative routines were underdeveloped. In addition,

4

Bossy and Delumeau take their long-range view because of a preference by many modern social historians (especially French ones) for history seen over long spans of time, combined with an emphasis on microscopic and local details and an interest in the impact of historical processes upon masses of ordinary and anonymous people. It is sometimes difficult to follow such historians in their pursuit of long-range factors, because many of us are limited to short, 'special periods' of history and so lack the background knowledge to move easily from medieval through early modern to modern times. But it is worth making the effort to understand a major historical process, such as the Counter-Reformation, that crosses the barriers between the conventional divisions of the historian's syllabus. In this pamphlet, therefore, there will be consideration of the late medieval background to the Counter-Reformation, and a look forward in time to its consolidation in the seventeenth and eighteenth centuries.

For all that, the pamphlet *will* concentrate heavily on the familiar central period of Catholic reform in the sixteenth century. Three main periods will be examined: the preparation of the Catholic reform in the late middle ages and early sixteenth century; the intensive work of the Counter-Reformation associated with the period of the Council of Trent, 1545–63; the protracted period of implementing the decisions made during the second half of the sixteenth century.

The origins of the Counter-Reformation

The alternative titles chosen for this pamphlet each indicate a particular approach to the subject. 'Counter-Reformation' suggests an aggressive Catholic attack on the Protestant Reformation. It also implies that the process of change and renewal in Catholicism would not have come about without the Protestant Reformation to stimulate the reform of the Catholic Church. One writer, Adolf Harnack, put this 'Counter-Reformation' viewpoint when he wrote that aspects of the Counter-Reformation were 'shadows of the Reformation', and that the Counter-Reformation amounted to 'a debt to the Reformation'. In contrast, the phrase 'Catholic

Reformation' points to deep and genuine restoration of Catholicism in the sixteenth century; the phrase indicates a spontaneous improvement in Catholicism. As might be expected, this 'Catholic Reformation' view has been favoured by Roman Catholic historians, such as the French writer Pierre Janelle, whose book has the deliberately chosen title, *The Catholic Reformation*. Another Catholic writer, H. O. Evennett, took the interesting middle position that a Catholic Reformation would have happened anyway, but that the nature of that Catholic Reformation was shaped by the Protestant Reformation and by the Catholic Church's desire to fight the Protestant Reformation. Another view is that religious Reformation in the sixteenth century was a varied thing. It was made up first of all of the Protestant Reformations in Germany, Switzerland, Scandinavia, England, Scotland, and so on. Second, it included a so-called 'Radical Reformation', which was more revolutionary than the main Protestant Reformation and which sought to recover the essence of the earliest Christianity. And, third, it took in the overhaul of the Catholic Church, as a 'Counter-Reformation' or 'Catholic Reformation'. Now when the roots of these Reformations – the Protestant, the Radical and the Catholic – are examined, it emerges that they all had a common origin: the Christian revival of the late middle ages. Thus we may say that the separate sixteenth-century Reformations were sub-divisions of a common experience – and, indeed, that they actually amounted to one Reformation. This statement may come as a surprise. After all, did not the various factions of Protestants, Radicals and Catholics accuse and denounce one another, curse one another, banish and execute one another? Yes, but in fact the conflicts of Christians in the sixteenth and seventeenth centuries were the violent quarrels of estranged members of the same family. All those quarrelsome brethren, their churches and sects, shared one common ancestor, which was the revived Christian piety of the two centuries before 1500.

In the middle of the 1300s Europe was stricken by plague on an entirely new and disastrous scale. In the wake of this 'Black Death', which killed perhaps a third of Europe's population, many European men and women turned for solace to the Christian religion. In doing so, they were showing a reduced confidence in

6

merely human solutions. Amongst some theologians, there was a revival of interest in the writings of the early Church father, Augustine of Hippo (354–430); in this revival thinkers stressed the power of Almighty God, the vanity of this world, the foolishness of human desires and thoughts, the need for God's gift of grace, and the need also to retire from the world, even while having to live and work in it. God was viewed as a figure of great power, a mighty judge. However, His son, Jesus, was a man like us and therefore was seen as a much more approachable figure, who was able to turn God's anger away from sinful man. As awareness of the humanity of Jesus Christ increased, He was actually seen as resembling late medieval man in all his sufferings. Some Italian artists depicted Jesus as an athletic 'superman', but painters from Germany and the Low Countries tended more to show Him as an infinitely wretched and anguished victim of mental and physical torment. Preachers, theologians and devotional writers emphasized the humanity of the suffering Jesus; Mary, His mother, was made a suffering mother to console, perhaps, all those parents who lost children in the awful epidemics of the late middle ages.

This stirring of emotional devotion in the late middle ages had a central focus in the cross of Christ, which became the common concern of all the sixteenth-century Reformations. The wave of piety in the late middle ages also directed people's attention to frequent prayer, meditation, the regular use of the sacraments of the Church, and pious reading; all these things were developed in the Counter-Reformation. Late medieval piety, especially in northern Europe, also give life to religious associations, especially for lay men and women in the everyday world. Such an association was the Brethren of the Common Life, founded by the fourteenth-century Dutch priest, Gerard Groote. In turn, the Brethren gave birth to an extraordinarily influential and poetic work of devotion, *The Imitation of Christ* (between *c.* 1390 and *c.* 1440). The piety movement encouraged aspirations that sought satisfaction in reform activity in the sixteenth century. We can trace a direct line between the personal religion expressed by the Brethren of the Common Life in such works as *The Imitation of Christ* and the fervent, emotive ('affective'), meditative and ascetic religion of the Counter-Reformation. Thus, Counter-Reformation piety was set out in works which can be compared to *The Imitation of Christ*, such as *Introduction to the Devout Life* by the French bishop, François de Sales (1567–1622), *Way of Perfection* and *Interior Castle* by the Spanish mystic, Theresa of Avila (1515–82) and even *Spiritual Exercises* by the Spanish founder of the Jesuits, Ignatius Loyola (1491–1556).

The Counter-Reformation also had its roots in the Italy of the Renaissance. The cultural explosion of the Italian Renaissance involved a return to the spirit of ancient Greece and Rome. In so far as this meant *pagan* Greece and Rome, there were Italian Catholics before the sixteenth century ready to denounce whatever was not Christian in the outlook of the Renaissance. These non-Christian elements in the Renaissance ethos were its love of physical human beauty, its glory in man and his achievements, its splendour, extravagance and aristocratic culture. These were attacked by the friar of Ferrara, Girolamo Savonarola, who exercised a hypnotic fascination over the cultivated city of Florence before his downfall and death in 1498. Savonarola heralded the Christian puritanism of the sixteenth-century Reformations. His vision of a pure and disciplined Christian city was fulfilled by John Calvin at Geneva between 1540 and 1564. The Savonarolan ideal of rigour and austerity in social life was implemented also in Rome itself by two popes of the Counter-Reformation, Paul IV (1555–9) and Pius V (1565–72).

The Italian preamble to the Counter-Reformation consisted both of the Renaissance and also of a Counter-Renaissance, expressed by Savonarola. The Counter-Renaissance gained ground because of another material disaster, which intensified the religious revival referred to above. This fresh catastrophe was the devastation of Rome in 1527 by Spanish and German troops – the Sack of Rome. This orgy of murder, torture, rape, plunder and sacrilege appeared to pious Italians in the light of a divine punishment and warning. For some years, Rome had been living out a heedless existence of debt, culture and extravagance, with hardly a thought for reform or salvation. Now the Sack of Rome in 1527 had a shock effect almost like that of the Black Death in 1348. For one Roman resident, Gian Matteo Giberti, the Sack of Rome initiated the Italian Catholic Reform as an active process. Already deeply pious, he was a senior, Rome-based ecclesiastical administrator, though officially bishop of the northern diocese of Verona where, after the Sack, he took up residence to make his see a model bishopric of the Counter-Reformation. Because of the importance of the Sack of Rome and the lead given by Giberti as a diocesan reformer, the real beginnings of the Catholic renewal can be traced to 1527. Bishops were the indispensable agents of the Counter-Reformation; the Council of Trent was largely their council, and they had the task of carrying out its requirements in the various parts of Europe. The systematic reform of bishoprics, parish by parish, involving the inspection of priests, the establishment of schools and seminaries, preaching and the administration of the sacraments, was the beating heart of the Counter-Reformation. The new commitment of the already pious Giberti to the active work of diocesan re-organization was important because he inaugurated, and provided the model for, a practical reform campaign by bishops in Italy. Giberti's dedication of himself to the restoration of the Church was also significant in that it represented a kind of religious conversion, in the sense of an intensification of religious experience, one that was in his case provoked by the Sack of Rome. In the transformation of his life around 1527 Giberti underwent a common sixteenth-century experience, shared, for example, by Martin Luther and Ignatius Loyola: an overwhelmingly forceful sense of personal religious renewal. None of the Reformations of the century can be properly understood without some knowledge of these accumulated individual religious regenerations. Europeans of all religious persuasions in the sixteenth century went through the same sequence of spiritual anxiety, nervous collapse and release by conversion as Martin Luther did.

The force of conversion is also seen in the life of Gasparo Contarini (1483–1542). Contarini was a member of a distinguished Venetian family, a diplomat, an engineer, a writer, a cardinal, a theologian, a reformer; his crisis of the soul was initiated by a friend's entry into a monastery (whereas Luther's anguish of spirit was accelerated by becoming a monk himself). Contarini described his spiritual difficulties in a passage which conveys the voices of the late medieval Church and of the Italian Renaissance at the point of transition to the early Counter-Reformation. The passage begins with Contarini sceptical about the efficacy of the saving mechanisms maintained by the medieval Church: 'Suppose I underwent every imaginable penance and more besides, that would still be insufficient to make me a great saint.' There Contarini is close to the mind of Martin Luther, in rejecting human aids to salvation. However, at this stage Contarini still manifested the outlook of the Renaissance in the quest for *virtú*, manly perfection in any area of endeavour. Part of Contarini still saw sainthood as a form of supreme artistry and human achievement, a goal, an ambition. He went on to speak of penances (in his case, self-inflicted punishments for sins) which 'would not compensate for my past misdeeds'. This was where Contarini renounced both the Renaissance pride in man and the late medieval Church's confidence in its salvationary provisions through indulgences and penances. Like Luther, Contarini came to believe that the solution to his problems lay in no human or ecclesiastical procedures but only in *grace*, that is the favour of God won through the merits of Christ on the Cross. This acceptance of saving grace was a common form of conversion for Christians in the sixteenth century. Many had lost confidence in their own efforts but trusted instead in the merits and benefits of Christ crucified. This subject involved some controversy in the Counter-Reformation Church: if the crucified Christ did everything to save sinful man, was there no place for man's co-operation, man's choice of the good, man's free will, man's good deeds? Contarini, and with him other Catholic reformers such as Cardinals Pole and Morone, tended to deprecate man's part in his redemption in favour of a stronger emphasis on redemption only through faith in what God had done in Christ for man; in this these 'evangelical' Catholic reformists were close to Luther's insights. In the end, after much controversy the Council of Trent, the authoritative Church council of the Counter-Reformation, determined that man played some part in his own redemption but nevertheless preserved some of the emphasis placed by Contarini, and even by the Lutherans, on the crucial saving work of Christ.

All the same, although Contarini denied that man could win

salvation through his own efforts, he did not believe in doing nothing. 'It is too difficult for a man of flesh and blood to renounce sense experience and turn to contemplation of God. . . . We must love and worship God in our neighbour.' Luther would have agreed. In this passage Contarini expressed the urge for action which the Counter-Reformation took over from the Renaissance. The release of the sinews of action is what we saw in the transformation of Giberti's career from one of prayer and contemplation to one of intense work. The same Renaissance humanist energy redirected into Christian channels can be seen in the work of three Counter-Reformation popes. Pius V (1565–72) rashly and constantly stirred up the politics of Europe and sought to purify the life of the city of Rome. Gregory XIII (1572–85) reformed the law of the Church, revised the calendar and directed the excavations of the catacombs. Sixtus V (1585–90) turned Rome architecturally into a capital city. This activism, allied to a conviction that God does all, is the key to the Counter-Reformation. It is brought to perfection in the saying of the Jesuits' founder, Ignatius Loyola: 'Work as if everything depended on you; pray as if everything depended on God.'

The stirrings of Catholic reform

We may distinguish two moods or phases of the Counter-Reformation. The first in time can be described as Italian, although Italians did not entirely monopolize it. It was protective and introverted, the initial reaction of serious-minded churchmen to the Protestant Reformation which broke out in Germany in 1517. They strove to preserve Italy from the 'contagion' of Protestantism by using the repressive mechanisms of the Inquisition and the Index of prohibited books. The Church adopted a defensive and frightened mentality appropriate to an institution that was being, so it seemed, reduced to its Mediterranean redoubts. The feeling of ecclesiastics that a serene and civilized Catholic order was being violated by barbarians can be seen in the 1520 bull of Pope Leo X against Luther, the 'wild boar' pillaging the Lord's vineyard of the Church. The pervasive siege mentality was apparently vindicated by the horrors of barbarian invasion in the form of the 1527

11

Sack of Rome, an event confirming fears of universal dissolution. Typical of this watchful, fearful mood was the reforming cardinal, head of the Inquisition, and later Pope Paul IV (1555–9), Giovanni Pietro Carafa. But the initial 'backs-to-the-wall' mentality was succeeded, during and after the Council of Trent, by a world-wide outlook in which defence gave way to confident attack and mission. Here again, Italians were prominent, but now the Counter-Reformation had become international. For example, in this second 'international' phase we see the Cardinal-Archbishop of Milan, Carlo Borromeo (1538–84), setting up a college to send missionaries to Switzerland to recover it all for Catholicism; we see English priests' training colleges (seminaries) opening up in Douai, Valladolid, Rome, Madrid and Lisbon in the hope of converting England back from Protestantism; and we see energetic missions, notably by the Dutch Jesuit, Peter Canisius (1521–97), to reconquer the German lands where the Protestant faith originated.

This point about the focus on Germany and Protestantism allows us to tackle the question, why was the process we know as the Counter-Reformation necessary, or seen to be necessary? For an answer we should move ten years on from the Sack of Rome to a document of 1537, *Report of a Select Committee of Cardinals on the Reform of the Church*. As we have seen, in its early stages from the 1520s to the 1560s the Counter-Reformation was primarily concerned with maintaining the Church's position in Italy, and was not as yet totally pre-occupied with Protestantism. This is brought home by the 1537 *Report of the Select Committee*. This report, commissioned by Pope Paul III, criticizes the Roman papacy with the utmost candour. It attacks superstition, the excesses of indulgence, prostitution in Rome, mercenary cardinals and the misuse of papal power, especially for money. But the survey was written by cardinals, who were officially the priests of the diocese of Rome, and that is perhaps why it is directed at Rome itself, rather than at Protestantism or the Church worldwide. Perhaps the cardinals felt that the repair of the Church's abuse must begin in its fountainhead, Rome. But the 1537 report evolved out of the immediate experience of its authors, and all these save one were Italians. True, the committee of nine cardinals shared amongst them considerable international training, but they had all been directly or indirectly affected by the trauma of the Sack of Rome considered as a Roman or Italian event, and specifically as warning chastisement. Although Italy's tragedy of the 1520s and of the whole long period of the Italian wars from the 1490s to the 1550s was brought upon her by foreigners, the events that concentrated the minds of Italians on the deficiencies of the Church did not take place outside Italy. Some years before, in the middle of the 1490s, the shock of French invasion had turned Florence away from worldliness and set her upon a course of religious reform under Savonarola. Now in the 1520s continued sufferings within Italy created an atmosphere of seriousness that forced senior churchmen to attend to the manifold ills of the Church. These cardinals did not reach the conclusion that Church reform was needed only because Luther and his followers had bolted from the Catholic Church. If disaster prompted Catholic reform, the disaster in question took place in Italy, with its wartime anguish, rather than in distant Germany. The need for extensive reform had long been apparent and had been voiced in Church councils in the fifteenth and early sixteenth centuries. It is true that the majority of the cardinals who produced the 1537 report shared attitudes concerning the means of salvation that were similar to Martin Luther's; that doubtless increased their appreciation of the need for Catholic Church reform, especially in matters like indulgences. More important, these reformist cardinals were products of the same contemporary reform mentality that produced Martin Luther in Germany, John Calvin in France, and Thomas Cranmer in England. In its turn the 'reform mentality' was engendered by the late medieval devotional revival, itself assisted by social crisis, which we considered in the second section of this pamphlet. Our awareness of those long-range and pervasive factors assisting a generalized reforming activity will enable us to dismiss as superficial any explanation of the Catholic Reformation as a simple reaction to the Protestant Reformation. Looking at the 1537 *Select Committee Report*, we can definitely say that the cause of the Catholic Reformation was not simply the Protestant Reformation.

As has already been indicated, the *Report of the Select Committee* was much concerned with the particular diocese of Rome. True, this was the world's most important diocese; but what the authors said about the renewal of this bishopric and the improvement of its bishop, the pope, applied to all Catholic dioceses, and the 1537 report certainly stimulated the thinking of the council fathers at Trent on the subject of reinvigorating the religious life of the bishoprics. The most important single feature of the Counter-Reformation is the cleansing, the disciplining, the inspection of the bishoprics. As we saw above, after the Sack of Rome, Bishop Giberti returned to his Verona diocese to set it in order. Non-Italian examples of the reformed dioceses can be found. In France, Bishop Guillaume Briçonnet (1472–1534) aimed to turn his diocese of Meaux into a model see by attracting scripture scholars and preaching gospel piety. Earlier, in a more spectacular and active way, the Cardinal Primate of Toledo, Francisco Ximénez de Cisneros (1435–1517), a Catholic reformer before the Reformation, envisaged the whole of Spain as one vast diocese to be reformed: he brought the religious orders back to observe their strict rules and raised the parish clergy to required standards of learning, sobriety and chastity. In the Low Countries, the beginning of Catholic reform can be dated to the reorganization of the area's bishoprics in 1559. But it was in Italy that the concept and the practice of reformed bishoprics reached its highest level.

Italy was suited to an unfolding series of Catholic Reformations, bishopric by bishopric, for three major reasons. First, it was not a united political state, but a mosaic of states; its highly developed framework of bishoprics fitted neatly into the highly decentralized political structure of the country. Also, Italians thought in regional terms: they expressed their strong sense of place with reference to parish or cathedral churches, and their reforming bishops became folk-heroes, especially because they were native Italians in the period after 1525 when so much of Italy was ruled by Spanish foreigners. Second, Italy was suited to reform by individual dioceses because of the characteristic Italian organization of the city-state and its governed territory (*contado*). In a city-state such as Florence the city itself, where the government was based, was the centre for a subject region of smaller

14

towns and villages. This form of political organization was reflected in the reform of the Italian bishoprics. For instance, in the reform of the archdiocese of Milan by Carlo Borromeo between 1565 and 1584, the archbishop as reformer was based in the city of Milan and functioned as the religious superintendent of the surrounding *contado*. Similarly, in the Bologna reforms of Cardinal Paleotti (1566–97) the territory was divided up for the purposes of religious reform into the city of Bologna, its suburbs and the countryside – again corresponding to the local political structure. Third, reform by dioceses was well suited to the Italian context because the Italians of the Renaissance had pioneered the concept of civic humanism. This was a set of ideals requiring service by the individual to the moral and educational renewal of the city considered as a community. The civic ideal, with a strong Christian tinge, can be seen in the career of Florence's unofficial leader between 1494 and 1498, the friar, Girolamo Savonarola. The goals of Christian civic humanism reached full realization during the Counter-Reformation period, in the lives and measures of two bishops of Rome, Popes Pius V and Sixtus V, and of two archbishops of Milan, Cardinals Carlo and Federigo Borromeo. These leaders fulfilled the Christian Renaissance ideal of unstinted and selfless service by the trained and educated leader for the good of the community as a whole. Tireless, self-denying, energetic, administrative, they attended to schools, universities and libraries, parish life and religious associations, the life and training of the clergy, the state of family and married life, poor relief, avoidance of luxury, waste and display, the suppression of prostitution, and to the encouragement of sobriety, even, with Sixtus V, architectural embellishment. The ideals of Savonarola were thus put into effect in the diocesan and urban reforms of the Counter-Reformation. The reforms involved a strong social discipline, but (as with Savonarola) the edge of harshness was taken off them by full charity provisions.

The priesthood

Diocesan reform implies reform by bishops, senior figures in the priestly establishment. To a great extent, the Counter-Reformation was a process implemented by priests and directed at the laity. It is sometimes salutary to be aware of the resemblances rather than the differences between the Reformations of the sixteenth century. But when we come to look at Counter-Reformation and Reformation views of ministry, we seem to find only dissimilarities.

The Counter-Reformation Church put the priest on a high plane, and distinguished carefully between the priest and the layman. This represented continuity with the state of affairs in the medieval Church, although in the middle ages the distinction between priests and people was often marked out by such priestly privileges as superior attainment of literacy over the laity. At the time of the Counter-Reformation the Church was faced with an implicit challenge to bring clergy and people into closer correspondence, as they were supposed to be aligned in the Protestant and Radical Churches. The Counter-Reformation resisted any challenge to draw the priest and the layman closer together, as it might have done, for example, by eliminating the rule of celibacy. But while preserving, and reinforcing, the differentiation between clergy and laity, the Counter-Reformation Church viewed the priest's differentness in rather altered ways from those of the middle ages. In the new era of the Church's history, the priest was to be marked out by professional training and performance of duties in a calling. Priesthood was more than ever made a vocation. In the process, the priesthood was coming to be considered as one of the professions, like the middle-class professions of law and medicine. However, the priest's monopolistic control of sacramental powers made his calling superior to any other. The sense of the priest as paternal ruler and guide of the laity suffused the Counter-Reformation. It can be seen, for instance, in the diocesan reforms of Cardinal Paleotti at Bologna, where a priestly civil service was created to control the diocese. The historian of these reforms in Bologna writes with surprise that Paleotti's priestly bureaucracy was advised 'occasionally even by laymen'. This concentration on the clergy is evident in the proceedings of the Council of Trent, which was a synod of clerics and which increased the sense of the Christian people as two peoples, priests and laity. The Counter-Reformation Church in fact envisaged an élite corps of highly disciplined and trained priests working for

16

the moral, spiritual and temporal welfare of the laity. The identification of the best in the Church with the priesthood and the religious orders can be seen in the way that the lives of pious lay people were approximated to those of clerics. Thus, when devout laymen became actively involved in the Catholic reform, they would tend to receive the priesthood, as Contarini did when Pope Paul III made him a cardinal in 1536.

This sense of the importance of the priesthood in the Church had two key aspects, both of them sharply intensifying medieval tendencies. One was the perception of the clergy as a separate order of mankind, different from the laity in training, dress, title and behaviour. The other was an even fuller acceptance than before of the prayers of the Church as being said by priests for, or on behalf of, the laity. In the Counter-Reformation, then, the emphasis on the distinctiveness of the clergy increased even above medieval levels. They were henceforward to be given a special training college formation. Of course, there had been cathedral schools in the middle ages, and the late fourteenth century diocesan statutes of St Andrews require clergy to attend annual 'refresher courses'. But the seminary of the Counter-Reformation was something different, a fully professional training.

We do not know the exact origins of the idea of the seminary. Perhaps it was devised in Granada in Spain; perhaps it was adopted from an experiment pioneered by Bishop Giberti in his Verona reforms; or perhaps it stemmed from a reform scheme of Cardinal Pole when he planned a 'seed-bed' (*seminarium*) for the training of priests. What matters is that the idea of a seminary, one in every diocese where there was no university, was taken up, endorsed and commanded by the Council of Trent. A key feature of the seminary was training in the art of preaching. Of course, it took a long time to implement the decree on setting up seminaries throughout the Church. Perhaps the seminary was a difficult venture to operate in any case: one took healthy boys on the brink of their teens and exposed them to an over-long and somewhat rigid education in theology, Church history and Latin. Probably the seminary boys had an unsatisfied appetite for more food and more play than they actually got. The bewildered priestly professors must have had great difficulty in providing for the boisterous tastes

17

of the very young. Nevertheless, some dismal aspects of the history of the seminary cannot conceal the fact that it gradually turned the Catholic priesthood into a professional corps of men who were more often than not faithful priests to the end of their days, though clearly some of them needed goading by bishops acting as supervisors. But sent out to the most benighted peasant parishes of Belgium, Poland, Italy and the rest, most of the ex-seminarians probably managed to retain the instilled professionalism of their early training: as the Council of Trent put it, they were 'formed in piety and religion at the tenderest age'.

Thus the seminary was the Council of Trent's most significant contribution towards raising priests with a proper appreciation of their priesthood. Priests were to be not simply better than lay folk: they were to be *different* from those around them. This difference, from the sixteenth century, was to be marked out by an even greater appreciation than previously of the need for a distinctive clerical dress. In addition, priests were supposed to be different from the laity in behaviour: grave, reserved, accessible but not affable, leading lives without sex, and, as regular instructions from bishops insisted, keeping out of wine shops and taverns. In fact, to the training of the seminary, which created habits and a strong sense of one's priesthood, was added the constant inspection and encouragement of those indispensable agents of the Counter-Reformation, the bishops, who were more free in the Counter-Reformation era than their medieval predecessors from secular government duties.

Priests emerged from the Counter-Reformation as one of the new or growing professions of the new age, along with Protestant ministers, doctors, lawyers, teachers, state servants, full-time soldiers and engineers. The Counter-Reformation was driven by a powerful urge to action. The good priest was not someone who simply *was* a priest; he was a distinctive type of person, specifically trained and fitted to perform priestly tasks. The model new priests, the Jesuits, rejected some venerable requirements of the past, such as harsh self-punishment for sins, or chanting prayers in choir, because those activities hindered doing and acting. What was the new-style Counter-Reformation priest required professionally to do? Three main areas suggest themselves: liturgy, preaching, and hearing confessions.

18

At the Counter-Reformation, the Catholic Church came to a crossroads over lay participation in worship, and reached those crossroads over the issue of language. The Council of Trent unequivocally decided to publish its revised liturgical documents only in Latin, especially the Mass-book (missal) issued by Pope Pius V after the Council's end in 1563; Latin and only Latin was to be the language of the Church's worship. In this case, as in others, the Counter-Reformation was looking for continuity with the medieval past as well as reacting against the Reformation demand for prayer in the language of the people. The Council's decision meant no change from the medieval procedure of the priest celebrating the Mass (the central prayer of the Catholic Church) on behalf of a congregation who could not generally follow its language. The priest continued to be the sole agent of the people in praying the Mass. With his back turned to the congregation for almost all the time, dressed in his squared-off 'Roman' chasuble (the priest's coloured over-vestment), using coded gestures, praying for most of the time silently and almost always in Latin, the priest was the ritual specialist, the professional pray-er of the people of God. What did those people do meanwhile? Perhaps there was less emphasis than there had been in the middle ages on the Mass as a rite of solidarity, reunifying and bringing peace to communities: the offering of a peace symbol, the *Pax*, was dropped out of the new rite. Perhaps the congregation was being gradually encouraged to follow the Mass as single individuals in private prayer. Alongside the Mass, new popular congregational prayer rites emerged at the time of the Counter-Reformation, as the medieval proliferation of masses for the dead was swept away. One of these new forms was Benediction, which was in a way derived from the Mass, and which involved blessing the congregation with a host of bread believed to be Christ. Another such rite was the exhibition that the Italians called *Quarant' Ore*, an occasional forty-hour long display of the host for worship. Perhaps strangely, the prayers at these popular devotions were also, like the Mass, set in Latin.

For all this talk of Latin in the rite, there was a time in the Mass when the priest used the language of the people. After the reading of the Epistle (usually one of St Paul's letters) and the Gospel (a selected passage from the New Testament account of Jesus), the priest was required to enter a raised open box, the pulpit, and, perhaps after reading some public notices, to preach a sermon, a short speech supposed to instruct the congregants in Christian doctrine and improve their morals. Sermon techniques had been developed in the middle ages, especially by the preaching orders of the Church, notably the Franciscan and Dominican friars. In fact, medieval preaching was rather a specialist activity, and parochial preaching was not universal: as late as 1549 a plan to improve preaching provisions in still-Catholic Scotland required each priest to deliver a sermon just four times a year. This all changed in the Counter-Reformation, and one of the ways in which the Protestant and Catholic Reformations resembled one another was in a heightened stress on preaching. In the sixteenth century Catholic Europe produced brilliant sermon-givers, many in the tradition of the intensely popular style of the saintly Philip Neri (1515–95). During his heyday, Neri dominated the religious life of the city of Rome as a kind of shadow pope for the common people. His preaching method, casual and informal, included what one French writer has termed 'burlesque'. A passionate pulpit oratory focusing on the death and benefits of Christ was the speciality of a friar who led the reformed Franciscan order of Capuchins, Bernardino Ochino (d. 1564). Not all parish priests of the Counter-Reformation era and its aftermath, of course, could come up to the standards of Neri and Ochino. Many parish priests must have been too shy or too tongue-tied to preach an uninhibited sermon. Many again must have used and re-used versions of the trial sermons they might have delivered to their fellow seminarians years before; while others perhaps employed standard books of stories and anecdotes to deck out their sermons. Or again, some probably spent their sermon time in bitter denunciations of their congregations' failings, or in repeated appeals for money for this, that and the other thing. For all that, in European societies which were making only halting steps towards mass literacy, the sermon, alongside the Sunday school and the First Communion class, was the most immediate way of teaching Christian doctrine to the populace. Many good sermons were preached, especially by the Jesuit fathers, who made a speciality of the practice. The importance given to this activity can be seen in the Catholic churches of Belgium, where the seventeenth-century carved oak pulpits, so fancifully shaped, are only slightly less imposing than the altars.

The third aspect of the Counter-Reformation priest's professional work is seen in the gradual adoption, throughout Catholic Europe from the late sixteenth century, of a new piece of church furniture: the 'confessional box'. Perhaps, as some have claimed, it was first introduced by Bishop Giberti in the Veronese reforms mentioned above. But the use of the 'confessional box' was certainly promoted by Milan's Archbishop Carlo Borromeo. Borromeo's purpose was to create the appropriate physical framework for an important sacrament of the Catholic Church, the sacrament of confession, or penance. Since about the twelfth century the Catholic Church had firmly upheld seven sacraments. These were held to have been founded by Christ and the Apostles; they were means and signs of the conveyance of grace (the gift of God so as to sanctify man) to the soul. Reformers like Martin Luther drastically reduced their number and function in the Protestant Churches. The Council of Trent, however, emphatically restated both the number of seven sacraments and their use. And, in particular, the Council confirmed the role of the sacrament of confession, whereby the individual sinner ('penitent') confessed his sins to a priest. That priest stood in for Christ and had the power to 'absolve' sins when they were sincerely confessed and repented, and when a penance was done for them.

After the Council of Trent, the actual manner of confession changed in a fashion which tells us much about the overall outlook of the Counter-Reformation. It tells us also about the new perception of the role of the priest. In medieval times, the penitent probably disclosed his sins to the priest in a whispered but semi-public meeting before Mass. The new 'box' for confession was a room in two sections with the priest ('confessor') and the penitent on either side of a grill through which one could speak but not see. This new piece of equipment in Catholic parish churches indicates a growing concern for confidentiality and spiritual intimacy. The Catholic Reformation grew up in an atmosphere in which many were extremely anxious about the precise state of their souls. The spiritual reading touched on earlier was concerned likewise with subjective, that is purely personal, states of mind and feeling. This seems to contrast with the general medieval outlook in which the sacrament of confession was probably more concerned with crimes against the community, acts of violence and so on. The attitude to confession in the Counter-Reformation did not of course overlook such social sins. But along with them, Counter-Reformation spirituality emphasized private or 'interior' sins. These were sins of thought and especially sexual offences against Catholic ethics, such as masturbation. Such sins, though they did no visible harm to the community, caused acute feelings of guilt. This guilt could be appeased in the privacy of the new confessional box.

To deal with the states of mind of individual penitents, the priest had to become a new kind of expert, a kind of analyst. Because of the expertise required for the task, the Council of Trent insisted that priests, to hear confessions, should have clear residential responsibilities for looking after souls, or should sit a special examination, or should give plenty of evidence that they could 'direct consciences'. Special skills were needed to hear confessions, different from those of the preacher. Extreme patience was required of those travelling 'missioner' confessors who listened to confessions from 6 to 11.30 am (with a break) and from 2 to 6.30 pm. These confessors were required to be as 'mild as lambs' to their penitents. They had to know, from long experience, how to deal with every different penitent, from the hard-headed cocksure to the over-sensitive, over-scrupulous worrier. Trained on 'cases of conscience' and pastoral theology, the father confessor emerged as an expert therapist. He was encouraged to use Carlo Borromeo's *Practice of Confession* and might even develop the doctrine of the Church along lines that would enable him to encourage his anxious penitents to believe in the probability of their being saved rather than damned. Some divisions of the clergy, especially the Jesuits, specialized in the difficult art of hearing confessions.

The Society of Jesus and other orders

The Society of Jesus ('Jesuits') was the most important new religious order of the Catholic Church to be founded in the

22

Counter-Reformation period. Its founder, Ignatius Loyola, should be considered, as were Giberti and Contarini, in terms of the widespread urge towards conversion amongst Catholics in the first period of the Catholic Reformation. In this context, 'conversion' does not, of course, mean a complete transformation from non-Christian; it means a bringing to life of religious fervour amongst baptized Catholics, and also the raising of any Catholic commitment already present in a person to a new level of intensity. Ignatius Loyola underwent a conversion in the sense of giving life to a formal commitment. As far as his religion was concerned, before 'conversion' Loyola (Iñigo Lopez de Loyola) observed the correct, stiff, inherited, orthodox, unthinking Catholicism of the Spanish knightly caste. What woke his faith was not a European catastrophe such as the Black Death, or an Italian disaster such as the Sack of Rome, but a local and more personal shock. When Ignatius was converted in 1521, it was not by the blows of the Protestant Reformation; his apparent unawareness of the German Reformation helps to demonstrate that the Catholic Reformation in the south was not brought into being by the Protestant Reformation in the north. The future founder of the Jesuits was transformed from formal religion to ardent piety by a spiritual crisis following upon a reading of a pious work after a disabling injury in a military skirmish in northern Spain in 1522. The piece of reading was *Vita Christi* (*The Life of Christ*) by Ludolph the Carthusian. The influence here was medieval; Ludolph belonged to a medieval religious order which specialized in the writing, copying and circulation of popular devotional works such as *Vita Christi*. Beyond Ludolph's work was the influence of the Spanish tradition of Catholic ardour, a tradition fed by Christian militancy in a country where Catholicism confronted Islam and Judaism. The belief in crusade was still strong in Loyola's country and was encouraged by the military cult of the national patron saint, James of Compostela. Soon after his conversion, Loyola expressed his new-found depth of faith in a perfectly medieval way, through a wish to undertake a mission of pilgrimage to the Holy Land.

Perhaps the Spanish influence on Loyola, and the traditions of his knightly class, come out most strongly in his use of military images. An early alternative name for the group of priests he brought together was the *Company of Jesus*, that is, as we might say now, the 'Jesus Regiment'. The leader was the 'General'. The constitutions were composed in what one writer has called a 'severe, soldier-like style'. Ignatius' methodically-organized meditations were entitled *Spiritual Exercises*, which could be rendered *Soul-drill*. We might, perhaps, be tempted to see in Loyola's use of a military style a hostile, fighting response to the Protestant Reformation. This is wrong, however; Ignatius seems to have thought very little about the Protestant Reformation. The military language came naturally to him because of his training as a soldier and because the traditions of Spanish Catholicism were those of the crusade. In any case, Loyola's employment of a soldierly language is a common Christian convention, stretching from St Paul, who urges us to 'put on the armour of Christ', through the early sixteenth-century reformist, Erasmus, who wrote a popular manual called *Handbook of a Christian Soldier* (*Enchiridion Militis Christiani*) to General Booth, the founder of the 'Salvation Army' in the nineteenth century.

But let us set aside the less familiar name of Company of Jesus in favour of the better known Society of Jesus. In 1534 Loyola, former soldier and then mature student, drew together a small group of companions, the nucleus of the future vast world-wide Jesuit order. The bringing together of like-minded pious people in religious fraternities is a most significant aspect of the Catholic reform. As a French historian of the Catholic Reformation, Daniel-Rops, writes: 'In various parts of Christendom and distinct from the larger formations, a number of priests would meet together for prayer and for mutual instruction with a view to the impending struggle on behalf of Christ; and some of such groups even bound themselves by religious vows.' A typical early group of this kind was a club that began meeting in Rome in the second decade of the sixteenth century. It called itself *'un Oratorio del Divino Amore'*, an Oratory of Divine Love, and it was probably a development of a pious association originating in Genoa. With numbers of about sixty, these associates would meet in a church in the Rome suburb of Trastevere for prayer and preaching. They were largely responsible for transforming the religious atmosphere of the city of Rome and they included notable reformers such as Giberti and Carafa. The latter, later Pope Paul IV, was, with the saintly Gaetano da Thiene, responsible for developing the *Oratorio* into a fully fledged religious order of the Church, the Institute of Clerks Regular, normally called Theatines. These Theatines became an enormously important religious order in the Counter-Reformation Catholic Church, first in Italy, then in Poland, Spain and Germany; they specialized in preaching and charitable work, and they are thought to have developed influential popular devotions such as the eucharistic adoration of *Quarant' Ore* ('Forty Hours') mentioned earlier.

The Jesuits evolved from an environment in which associations were formed of people with ideas and attitudes in common, and they also proceeded to form their own religious societies. Having rapidly emerged as prominent educators – in the 'Franco-Belgian' province there were 5,600 students in Jesuit schools in 1643 – the Order created 'sodalities' of its former students – who totalled some 11,300 in the Franco-Belgian province in 1640. Among these sodalities can be found leaders of secular and professional society in Catholic Europe. In Belgium, for instance, the artists Van Dyck, Rubens and Teniers were all Jesuit sodality members.

The orders of 'clerks regular' such as the Jesuits and Theatines came out of a matrix of pious sodalities and they projected such pious societies forward into the Catholic world. Devout societies had a long history going back into the middle ages. Some of these societies, such as the Third Order of St Francis ('Tertiaries'), had some characteristics of religious orders, but were designed for Christians living in the lay world. A useful collective name for these medieval religious organizations is 'confraternities', in other words close gatherings of brethren in religion. In the Counter-Reformation period the traditional confraternities were put under close priestly control, and were reorganized as 'archconfraternities'. In the Milan archdiocese Carlo Borromeo investigated and regulated a long-standing local religious society, the *Humiliati*, founded in a wave of apostolic enthusiasm in the middle ages but now alleged to be 'degenerate'. The increased priestly supervision of the religious societies was part of the process of clericalization of the Catholic Church which was noted above. But the process was not all one way. In taking on active functions, in preparing themselves for the priesthood by seminary training, in doing work requiring expertise, in dispensing with certain time-consuming and 'monastic' practices such as singing joint prayers, the 'new' priests of the Counter-Reformation, and especially those, like the Jesuits and Theatines, called clerks regular, unconsciously approached the ethos of the laity, especially the middle-class and professional laity. There was a continual interaction between Church and world, with the 'sodalities' or 'archconfraternities' helping to take the Church into the world, and the new orders taking the world into the Church.

The popular impact of the Counter-Reformation

How could the orders and the priesthood of the Catholic Church have an impact on the world? The Jesuits' role as educators has just been mentioned. One of the ways in which they triumphed as teachers was in fostering drama. The 'college dramas' of the Jesuits are justly famous. In 1624 they put on *The Life of St Francis Xavier* in faraway Goa, and they produced *The Triumph of David* in the Tamil language of the south of India. In France the Jesuit drama reached a point of perfection in the work of their pupil, the tragedian Pierre Corneille (see especially his martyrdom drama, *Polyeucte*, 1643).

However, the main point about drama, in the present context, is that there is only a thin dividing line between the sermon and the play. In the middle ages, plays – miracle plays, morality plays, passion plays – grew out of the data of bible history. At the same time, preachers themselves developed dramatic methods. The two chief preaching squadrons of the medieval Catholic Church, the orders of Franciscans and Dominicans, dressed theatrically, in habits of grey and black on white. These professional preachers were accomplished artists of the theatre, at a time when the frontier between life and art had not been firmly drawn. They perfected cadences of the voice and gestures of the hands to make their points. One of them, it is said, would, in an entirely theatrical style, throw a sandal at a sleeping member of his congregation. Though lacking a gift for broad comedy, the Dominican Savonarola, in so many ways the herald of the Counter-Reformation, was an accomplished pulpit actor. These preaching art-forms reached perfection in the period of the Counter-Reformation, when the Catholic Church used histrionics (i.e. techniques relating to the stage) as one of its many devices for making a popular impact on a Europe that was drifting away. Perhaps its supreme artist, the saint as clown, was Rome's Philip Neri. This 'mystic in motley' would wear his clothes inside out, deliberately bring grammatical mistakes into the prayers of the Mass, dance on the altar, imitate a drunk, fall into talk and laughter with any stranger on the street. His humour may not appeal to our modern world, but it was effective in its own time because it belonged to the Italian city and popular culture of the later middle ages, to the world of jesters and street satire; it belonged also to the developing styles of the Italian *commedia dell'arte*, the popular theatre.

In other respects, though still in pursuit of a popular impact, people in the forefront of the Counter-Reformation would use more serious approaches. Another order of clerks regular, the Clerks Regular of St Paul ('Barnabites') first appeared in the streets of Milan with ropes around their necks, carrying huge crosses and stopping periodically to preach God's love. The reformed order of Franciscans established as 'Franciscan Hermits' ('Capuchins') by Matteo da Bascio in 1528 made a particularly sensational impact because of the drama of their costume. They were clad in the coarsest material in a habit which, it was claimed, was the exact replica of that of St Francis of Assisi. These friars deliberately went shoeless in all weathers, and with their unkempt beards and great square hoods they caught the imagination of the people of the streets who promptly nicknamed them *I Capucini*, the hooded men. Perhaps the high point of Capuchin dramatics came in the Low Countries in the seventeenth century when as preachers they entered churches with lists of their own sins pinned to their backs.

Was all this pure artistry? It depends on our definition of art. If we mean by art pure beauty for its own sake, then the Counter-Reformation had no such conception. One neat summary of the artistic outlook of the Council of Trent concludes that 'the Church encourages veneration of artistic works which allow the

27

faithful to strengthen their belief with beautiful forms'. So Counter-Reformation art was functional and subservient; that is, the arts were intended to elevate religion, which they served. This functional view of art makes it difficult for us to decide where religion ends and art begins. Were the mystical masterpieces of Theresa of Avila and her poet contemporary, John of the Cross (1542–91) literature or devotion? And if St Theresa herself was an artist, what do we make of the artist who sculpted her – Gian Lorenzo Bernini (1598–1680)? Bernini was in many ways a holy layman: he received holy communion once a week, and once a year went on a retreat (a spiritual withdrawal from the world for a period of silence and prayer). In his celebrated *Ecstasy of St Theresa* (1645), the last thing Bernini set out to create was simply a beautiful work of art as we might now understand the term. Instead, he was depicting as accurately as he could in sculpture the ineffable and sublime mystical experience which St Theresa in her writings had compared with physical sensations.

Bernini has, indeed, been aptly described as 'the personification of the Catholic Reformation'. He certainly was a brilliant publicist for it. In works such as *The Chair of St Peter* and the *baldacchino* (the canopy on spiral columns) in St Peter's Basilica, Rome, Bernini's art was intended to teach that the Roman papacy was guided by the Holy Spirit and that the Catholic Church was the direct descendant of the temple of Solomon in the Old Testament (also believed to have such spiral columns). It is not surprising that Bernini read every night from St Ignatius Loyola's *Spiritual Exercises*. This book required the meditating Christian to be as concrete and realistic as possible. If the meditant were thinking, for instance, about the birth of Christ, then, according to the so-called 'Ignatian method' set out in the *Spiritual Exercises*, he should 'consider the cave, where it takes place, and how large, how small, how low, how high it was; how it was furnished'. As with medieval Christian art, Counter-Reformation religious art, such as that of Bernini, had as its primary purpose the functional assistance of prayer and contemplation.

The point that Counter-Reformation artists functioned as preachers, while religious figures behaved like artists, is not restricted to Bernini and St Theresa. It applied equally to those saints who operated within a genre, a repeated style. For instance, Carlo Borromeo deliberately patterned himself on his predecessor as Archbishop of Milan, St Ambrose, and Philip Neri made himself like St Francis of Assisi. Saints like Borromeo and Neri were essential to the success of the Counter-Reformation: to return to the analogy between drama and preaching discussed above, they were its 'stars'. In their lives they personified and exemplified the ideal qualities of Counter-Reformation Christianity, and their 'star quality', which gave them such great popular influence during their lives, making them 'cult figures', was recognized after their deaths by their canonization.

Thus, Theresa of Avila, Ignatius Loyola and the Jesuit missionary, Francis Xavier, were all canonized together in a great ceremony at St Peter's, Rome, in 1622, in what was a triumphant celebration of the spirit of the Counter-Reformation. Carlo Borromeo, who in his active life fulfilled what the German historian of the Counter-Reformation, Hubert Jedin, described as the 'bishop-ideal' of the Catholic Reform, had already been canonized in 1610. Such saints, and other heroes of the Counter-Reformation such as François de Sales (canonized 1655) or Roberto Bellarmino (canonized 1930), all had in common the characteristics of energy, organization and efficiency. It has been said of St Theresa in particular that she 'combined the life of religious contemplation with an intense activity and common-sense efficiency in "practical" affairs'. The energy and practicality which Theresa showed in founding and organizing convents throughout Spain was also conspicuous, of course, in Ignatius Loyola. As General, he acted as co-ordinator of the early Jesuit order, especially in the mission field. Loyola's attention to practicality and efficiency can be seen in his avoidance of harsh discipline. As Jean Delumeau has described it, a vast and silent revolution took place in early modern European life, which promoted method, planning, preparation, practicality, energy and application. The Counter-Reformation played a key part in this 'rise of efficiency'. It can be seen, for instance, in the Church government reforms of the period, especially those of Pope Sixtus V (1585–90), with his creation of 'congregations' (i.e. ministries), each having a competence over a particular aspect of the life of the

Church. Loyola's attitude is echoed by other saints of the epoch. The brilliant organizer, Vincent de Paul (*c.* 1580–1660), told the nursing sisters under his charge, 'looking after the sick is praying'. Camillo de Lellis (1580–1614) was another saint of the sick ward, with a medical orderly's care for method, system and effort rather than contemplation or self-deprivation. He once threatened to sack a nursing brother who wished to chastise himself by sleeping on firewood; the efficient performance of the job in hand was more important, indeed more meritorious. As a male nurse, de Lellis insisted that the wards be washed, the patients' records maintained, the patients kept clean, contagious diseases isolated. In this way, de Lellis and his kind were typical both of the dawning 'age of efficiency' and of the practical spirituality of the Counter-Reformation.

Success and failure in the Counter-Reformation

Was the Counter-Reformation a success? To answer, or even address, this question we shall have to take a long view. The process was not over in the period 1563–1622; in some regions, as Delumeau shows, it had hardly even begun by the latter date. But the effort to assess the success of a movement so broad and long lasting as the Counter-Reformation obviously involves formidable problems. For example, the Catholic Church's main aim during the Counter-Reformation (as indeed throughout its history) was to ensure that as many souls as possible reached heaven. It is quite clearly impossible for us to evaluate success or failure in this area! Therefore we cannot say how successfully the Counter-Reformation achieved its own chief aim. All we can say is that leading Counter-Reformation figures probably did think that the Church was more successful in this task than in the past; but at any arbitrarily chosen point in the Counter-Reformation, say the end of the seventeenth century, churchmen would almost certainly have believed that much more needed to be done.

If we cannot count souls in heaven, what *can* we count? We could try to reconstruct numbers of people who attended Mass over the long Counter-Reformation era. We could count (historians regard this as particularly telling) the number of people in a locality who made 'Easter duties' (that is, received the sacraments of Confession and Holy Communion at least once a year). Where available, the figures for individual locations might be astonishingly high, especially when compared with the data that are available for the middle ages. But this is where we encounter one of those problems that bald statistics, even when they are complete, often present. If the people were there in church, did they *want* to be? Were they dragooned there by conformity, by the village herd instinct, by respectability or, worst of all, by the busybody activities of local magistrates seeking to impose 'social control' through religion? And if the people were attending church, what was going on in their heads when they were there? We cannot be sure, but it is clear that the chief agents of the Counter-Reformation set themselves the task of instructing the people more fully than their medieval ancestors had been in Catholic doctrine. Were they successful in that? The remarks of a French priest, made in about 1700, when the Counter-Reformation should have made some headway, suggest that ancestral beliefs survived strongly. 'There are some [amongst his parishioners] who harbour ancient errors in their hearts which they justify only by saying that their fathers thought this, and which they silently abide by. For example, that one may be saved in any religion.' That completely contradicted official Catholic teaching, and these parishioners were, strictly speaking, heretics. This disturbing disclosure underlines what some historians now suspect: that beneath a surface conformity of belief, the peoples of Catholic Europe manifested a number of departures – 'ancient errors' – from the orthodox teaching of the Catholic Church. It is a perception which is strongly supported in a marvellous book by an Italian historian, Carlo Ginzburg, *The Cheese and the Worms*. If we were to develop this idea, it might be along the following lines. From the start of the Counter-Reformation, the Catholic Church, in co-operation with state authorities, overcame ancient popular dissent and negligence and imposed outward conformity of belief and practice on a recalcitrant population. When that population got the chance, at the time of the French Revolution (1789 onwards) or at the time of the Industrial Revolution (1780 onwards), it threw off the Catholic religion and became voluntarily

31

'de-Christianized'. There are flaws in this theoretical argument, and it is not accepted in this pamphlet; but it should at least be thought about.

The French parish priest whose comments were quoted shared in a common opinion that to be a Christian one had to subscribe to a list of 'correct' beliefs in a central corpus of doctrine. But if we take another possible criterion – the Christian practice of charity – the priest's remarks seem to show a very high level of Christianity among his parishioners: 'one may say of almost the entire parish that they have great charity for the poor.' Thus perhaps it may be suggested that the greatest success of the Counter-Reformation (so far as the people of Catholic Europe were concerned) was in producing a population with a strong and active sense of Christian ethics. The bishops, priests, nuns and religious orders who implemented the Counter-Reformation set themselves the large task of producing a better-behaved population than had inhabited Europe in the middle ages: less violent and prone to feuding, more sober and chaste, more industrious and better educated. Did they succeed? It is too vast a question even to be attempted. Though paralleled by the work of Protestant pastors and magistrates, the Counter-Reformation was the most ambitious campaign of mass indoctrination, in behaviour as well as belief, ever to be attempted in European history. On the most obvious level, it implied schooling, guided by the Jesuit principle of the formation of the adult through the early education of the child. As well as the schools of the Jesuits, there were, for example, the girls' schools of the Ursuline Sisters, and the schools for the poor founded by the Canon of Rheims, Jean Baptiste de la Salle (1651–1719). But the education of Europeans in Catholicism meant more than schooling: it meant the sermons and sacraments, the processions and missions, the works of art, the baroque churches. The success of the Counter-Revolution also implied formal political processes which we will examine next.

The politics of the Counter-Reformation

As we have seen, the Counter-Reformation owed its success mainly to persuasion, indoctrination and all the forms of propaganda (a word that was actually coined in the Counter-Reformation). But before the operatives of the Counter-Reformation could enter districts to win or win back their peoples to the Catholic religion, territories had to be reclaimed for Catholicism in the formal and political sense of declaring the allegiance of their rulers and peoples to the Roman Church. Of course, a number of lands, chiefly in northern Europe, having gone over to the Reformation in the sixteenth century, were never to be regained by the Catholics. By the same token, lands in the Mediterranean south were hardly ever in doubt as to their choice of religion in the sixteenth century, though pockets of dissent were eliminated and the Catholicism of the southern countries was consolidated and intensified during the Counter-Reformation. Spain and Italy were in fact the springboards for the re-Catholicization of a crucial band of territories – debateable lands – where a great deal of the energy of the Counter-Reformation was invested politically, militarily and educationally, first in restoring or clarifying the official links between those countries and Rome and then in deepening the attachment of their peoples to Catholic faith. These lands, which wavered between Catholicism and Protestantism in the sixteenth century, but which were recovered for Catholicism at various times from about 1560, included France, Belgium, Austria, Bavaria, Bohemia and Poland. This was a wide band of vital border countries running from east to west, much of it on the frontier between the mostly Catholic south and the predominantly Protestant north. France, above all, held the key to the balance of power between the rival religions in early modern Europe; there, the outcome was decided, before the end of the sixteenth century, by military and political factors and by the persisting strength of Catholic opinion. Likewise, in Germany and central Europe the Catholic recovery was engineered by political manipulation in the late sixteenth and early seventeenth centuries; subsequently, the restoration of Catholicism was essayed on the battlefield in the catastrophic Thirty Years War of 1618–48, concluding in the stalemate of the 1648 Peace of Westphalia. As in central Europe, so across the Continent, the balance of forces established between the rival forms of Christianity by the middle of the seventeenth century has proved durable, with minor adjustments, down to our own day.

France was racked by religious civil wars from the 1560s to the 1590s. At the end of the religious wars, the leader of the Protestant coalition, Henry of Navarre, was converted to Catholicism and became King of France as Henry IV. In part, Henry was thus paying tribute to the apparently ineradicable Catholicism of the great majority of French people. As king, Henry IV developed a strong Catholic commitment, bringing in the Jesuits and making one of them his confessor. The end of the religious wars in France was sealed by a treaty between the religious factions, the Edict of Nantes (1598). This peace of exhaustion gave the French Protestants (Huguenots) a guaranteed position in French life, and freedom of worship. Thus the Edict can be said to have weakened the traditional role of the Catholic Church in France. However, the Nantes Edict was signed on the eve of a dramatic Catholic revival in France. The Protestant minority was threatened by this revival; the Jesuits captured some of the commanding heights of French education; members of the Protestant nobility, whose support had been indispensable to the cause during the Wars of Religion, were converted to Catholicism. Throughout the period 1598–1685 the Huguenot community was weakened in numbers and morale. In 1685, by revoking the Edict of Nantes, Louis XIV was effectively declaring that his kingdom had been recovered for the Catholic faith.

In the southern Netherlands (today's Belgium), political factors decided the religious outcome. As in neighbouring France, this part of Europe was the scene of religious strife within communities. Elements of the population, led by dissident nobles, sought to reject the overlordship of Spain and its king, and these elements were joined by, or fused with, those who wished to throw off Catholicism and introduce the reformed brand of Protestantism ('Calvinism'). In the late 1570s political radicalism under Calvinist auspices in the south Netherlands produced a conservative reaction, especially amongst the governing classes, in favour of the Spanish monarchy and Catholicism; from about 1580 Spain's General, the Prince of Parma, exploited this political and religious backlash so as to retrieve the provinces for Spain. Though the long-term goal of Parma and of Spain's Philip II and his successors to regain the whole Netherlands was thwarted, in 1598 Spain was able to put the southern provinces under the government of the Spanish-backed 'Archdukes', who ruled from Brussels and who sponsored the complete re-Catholicization of the area. Much movement of population took place, Protestants from the towns and villages of these now Catholic south Netherlands migrating to the independent and Protestant north. The Jesuits set to work in the south Netherlands; architectural and artistic restoration began and came to a climax in the Catholic baroque work of Peter Paul Rubens and Anthony van Dyck. Belgium emerged in the seventeenth century as the showpiece of the Catholic Reformation in northern Europe.

For over half a century the situation in Germany was stabilized and peace maintained by the Peace of Augsburg of 1555. This truce of the religions allowed Catholic and Lutheran regional rulers to make the ultimate decisions about the religions to be accepted in their territories. In southern Germany the result of the Augsburg truce was to favour the return of Catholicism. In Austria and Bavaria the Counter-Reformation drove out earlier Protestant influences from the 1560s onwards. Regional rulers such as dukes Albert V and William V of Bavaria, and Ferdinand of Austria implemented tough policies to eliminate Protestantism and promote reformed Catholicism. The political authority of such rulers was increased by their furthering the Catholic faith. These princes gained ground over Protestant noblemen and over the estates (local parliaments) in which Protestant opinions had been voiced up to about 1563. In these Catholic lands of Germany, the Counter-Reformation rulers gained increased authority over the Church itself, as part of their price or reward for forsaking Lutheranism, which tended to put regional churches under the presidency of 'godly princes'. Albert of Bavaria acquired the authority to introduce the measures of the Council of Trent in his lands, and a grateful Pope Pius IV granted him rights to 10 per cent of clergy income in Bavaria.

The restitution of Catholicism in German lands was made possible, of course, by other factors apart from political decisions. The preaching work of Peter Canisius had great results. His *Catechism* (question-and-answer book) of Christian doctrine influenced generations of German Catholics. The Jesuits founded famous schools and colleges at key centres such as Ingolstadt, Vienna and Cologne, and these acquired such high prestige that Protestant parents sent their children to them. It was soon noted that Catholic children in the Jesuit schools were vastly more pious than their parents: a generation gap opened up in the first period of the German Catholic recovery between the tepid Catholic morale of the period 1520 to 1560 and the intense zeal of the German Counter-Reformation.

The Catholic Church held on to much of Germany through its retention of the 'ecclesiastical territories', the German lands that were ruled politically by bishops. After much vacillating, the territory of Cologne was kept for Catholicism, and with it Mainz and Trier, giving the Catholic Church an important spearhead in the Rhineland and Westphalia.

Flushed with increasing confidence, the Catholic side in Germany grew more and more aggressive in the early seventeenth century; a series of disquieting incidents on the borders between the two faiths endangered the fragile Augsburg truce, while the aim of the now assertively Catholic Habsburg House of Austria to restore its grip on a kingdom of Bohemia permeated by Protestant influences led to war in 1618. However, the outcome of the Thirty Years War showed that in Germany the decisions of territorial dynasties were more influential than military events in deciding religious allegiances.

In Bohemia re-Catholicization was largely an imposed process after 1620. It involved the extirpation of the old, pre-Reformation Hussite tradition, the deportation of Czech Protestants and the control of education by the Jesuits. In Poland a dramatically successful conversion of a multi-faith land into a single-faith Catholic territory was achieved through the support of the Polish kings Henry Bathory (1576–86) and Sigismund III (1587–1632), through the episcopal Catholic reformism of Cardinal Stanislaus Hosius (d. 1579) and by building on the base of Polish peasant allegiance to Catholicism. The consequences of this recovery are still evident today.

In the areas discussed in this section, the agents of the Counter-Reformation conducted a mission of recovery, assisted by favourable political and military factors. Outside Europe, the

Counter-Reformation Church conducted a mission of new conversions. Let us now look at that extension of the work of the Counter-Reformation.

Missions

First a group of quotations:

> Even the form in which Christianity is preached in Asia, Africa and the Indies is incredible if not ludicrous: an odd coloured man in funny clothes, perspiring, with a flushed face, speaking the language badly or not at all, wanting his hearers to abandon everything they hold sacred, their traditional beliefs, their culture, institutions, even their families, to subscribe to a doctrine that his fellow whites barely pay lip service to.
>
> (Edward Rice, *The Great Religions*)

> The monarchs of Castile sent us not to subjugate you, but to teach you the true religion.
>
> (Christopher Columbus, to the natives of Haiti)

> In asking Pope Alexander VI to grant us ownership of half the islands and mainlands of the Ocean, our definite purpose was to use all our efforts to induce the peoples of these new lands to embrace our holy religion, to send them priests, monks, prelates and other learned and God-fearing men who would educate them in the truths of the faith, and to give them the manners and customs of Christian life.
>
> (From the *Testament* of Isabella, Queen of Spain)

> We consider . . . that they really are men, and not only capable of understanding the Catholic religion but according to our information exceedingly desirous of embracing it.
>
> (From the bull *Sublimis Deus* of Paul III, 1537)

Each of the quotations underlines the fact that the foreign missionary activity of the Catholic Church in the entire Counter-Reformation period had social, political and cultural implications. Put another way, the Counter-Reformation mission cannot be seen entirely in spiritual terms. Mr Rice caustically and amusingly accuses the missionary of attempting to wipe out native cultures. Columbus tried to persuade the Antilles Indians that the arrival of the Spanish meant the preaching of the Christian faith, which was quite separate from loss of political independence. The remarks of Isabella the Catholic point to a cultural and educational mission to the Indians in which a higher culture – the Spanish – would indoctrinate primitive peoples into the mysteries of superior civilization: 'educate them in . . . the manner and customs of Christian life'. Pope Paul's strange remark, which needs explaining – 'they really are men' – was meant to end a debate as to whether the American Indians were fully-fledged human beings. The pope is saying that the Indians *can* respond to teaching, and also that they must be treated humanely, that is, not enslaved nor otherwise ill-treated.

The question of the relationship between the spread of Counter-Reformation Christianity and the survival of the cultures of the non-European world is an intricate one. It is a question that is related to the interaction of Counter-Reformation religion and the popular culture of Europe itself. With a few brilliant exceptions, such as Fathers de Rhodes (1591–1660), di Nobili (1577–1656) and Verbiest (d. 1688), the priests and friars who went to America, India, Japan and Africa could not escape from their European backgrounds. They could hardly stop themselves being Europeans, making European assumptions. One of these assumptions is seen in the cheerful confidence shown by the majority of the missionaries in the superiority of their continent's civilization. Therefore, they had no hesitation about teaching European culture as they taught Christianity. This culture trap, however, obstructed the successful implementation of Christianity in many parts of the non-European world.

We shall soon look at some random numbers of converts. First, though, let us ask two questions about the Counter-Reformation missions. Why did the missionaries bother and why did the natives convert? The first question is not as obvious as it seems. After all, it was the Catholics who conducted the missions we are discussing. Protestants were not particularly to the fore in the mission to the heathen. Luther seems to have seen mission in terms of a campaign to cleanse the Church. In countries like

England the Protestant version of mission was a crusade to make home society holy or 'godly'. We might say that the reason that Catholic states like Spain and Portugal conducted missions was that they were simultaneously founding huge empires which they had duties to christianize. This argument does not hold water. After all, the Protestant English and Dutch founded empires but did not show the missionary enthusiasm of the southern Catholic states. In any case, Catholic missions were conducted in lands such as China and Japan where there was little real hope of a European imperial presence.

So the 'colonial' theory of the Catholic mission does not stand up to inspection. Another theory to explain the Catholic missions from the sixteenth century could be labelled the 'compensation' theory. This theory has much more credibility inasmuch as Catholic commentators in the seventeenth century actually said that the Catholic faith was making up for losses of people in Europe with gains overseas.

Although the 'compensation' theory is a valuable one, one might argue that the real reason for the upsurge in Catholic missionary fervour from the sixteenth century onwards was the mood and mentality of the Catholic Church in the so-called Tridentine era. Catholics after Trent developed an extraordinary assurance in the rightness of the Catholic faith. If it was actually true that there was 'no salvation outside the Church', then it was the highest work of charity to bring the pagan into the Church. Missionary work may have been clumsy, as Mr Rice points out, but there was no escaping its imperative. We are looking at the Catholic missions here, in this overall study of the Catholic Reformation, because they arose necessarily from the fervour, the zeal, of the Catholic Reform.

If the missionaries brought a message, they elicited a response. Why did the natives of the extra-European world accept the Christian faith from the missionaries? One way of answering that question of course is to say that the natives did not convert to Catholicism. This is where we should look at our random figures. Take China, for instance. China in the sixteenth century had an estimated population of 75 million. By the time of the death of the missionary Matteo Ricci in 1610, only 25,000 Chinese had been baptized. (But, to be fair, the number of new conversions was up to 200,000 by 1700.) In Japan, with a smaller population, progress was more impressive and by the 1590s the Japanese islands probably contained 300,000 converts. However, Japan's 'Christian period' was brief; a political reaction virtually extinguished the Catholic Church in Japan by 1640. But playing the numbers game does not get us out of tackling the question – why did the inhabitants of the non-European world convert to the 'European religion', Catholicism? The numbers *alone* are not too significant. In the persecutions of the 1630s of Japanese Christians by the *Shoguns* (dictators), perhaps 37,000 were put to death for their Christianity. The numbers are impressive; even more impressive is the commitment of those Japanese who were Christianized enough to undergo martyrdom.

In any case, a head count of newly baptized Catholic Christians outside Europe will in fact show up some large numbers. In Latin America there are some sensational conversion figures, often achieved by solitary missionaries. For instance Bishop Toribio de Mogrovejo boasted in 1594 that he had confirmed half a million people in western South America. In a new mission to the Apaches, the Jesuits had, by 1630, performed 80,000 baptisms.

So we must return to the question: why did 'natives' accept Catholicism in the Counter-Reformation period? Possible answers include coercion, prestige and persuasion.

First coercion. Undoubtedly this was applied. The Spanish in South America perpetrated savage atrocities on the native people. These atrocities were narrated by a Dominican missionary, himself a Spaniard, Bartolomé de las Casas, in his *Brief Relation of the Destruction of the Indians*; in this work the friar accused his own people of genocide in South America. We hear the plaintive cry of the Indian being tortured by the Spanish: 'the torments inflicted upon us are much worse than any that could be devised by all the devils in hell.' Apart from direct violence, there were clumsy attempts at wholesale conversion by the Spanish pioneers in South America, the 'Conquistadores'. As they passed rapidly through native villages, these soldier-explorers would frequently mass-baptise whole tribes without instruction. Then, when the bondage system called *encomienda* was established in South America as a form of estate slavery, the natives were dragooned into Catholicism. However, it is questionable whether any of these forceful methods of 'conversion' was really effective in depth, and they were often counter-productive. That is to say, Spanish methods often eliminated rather than converted native peoples, and those who were forcibly made into Catholics were reluctant, resentful and insincere in their attitudes, associating their new religion with conquest, servitude, exploitation and inhumanity. It may be that under Catholic forms pre-Christian beliefs survived in the Indians of South America; it is even sometimes suggested that the Catholic Church in Latin America acted only as a transplanted institution for European colonials and their descendants. So as not to leave this subject only with a distorted impression, a 'black legend' of Spanish Catholic brutality in South America, it is worth mentioning the efforts of missionaries to check exploitation, and the extraordinary experiment in social care for the Indians run by the Jesuits in their 'reduction' of Paraguay in the eighteenth century.

Whatever conclusions we reach about the efficacy of coercion in propagating Catholicism in South America, force such as was exerted in the Spanish colonies cannot possibly explain missionary success in the Far East, where the missionaries enjoyed no political influence. There (as in South America) we can examine our second theory to account for Catholic missionary success: prestige. Consider the impact of the Spanish Conquistadores, with their guns and horses, on the inhabitants of the sub-continent. Or consider this question asked by some missionaries of prospective converts in India: 'Do you wish to enter the caste of the *Prangui* (Portuguese)?' In this case the missionaries hoped to make gains by liberating the lower caste from the rigid Hindu system. Clearly, the missionaries took advantage of a widespread admiration of them as cultural and technological supermen. It is significant that the missionary to China, Matteo Ricci, was called by the Chinese themselves the 'foreign magician'. Some of the missionaries to China impressed natives because of their command of skills that were incidental to the teaching of Christianity. The Jesuit Johann Adam Schall von Bell managed the Chinese emperor's observatory, reorganized the calendar and advised on the fortifications of Peking. Until 1767 the Jesuits ran the emperor's observatory. However, in these cases the technical ability of the missionaries as mathematicians, astronomers, even watchmakers, may have taken precedence in the minds of their hosts over their missionary activity.

The answser to our question about the acceptance of the Christian gospel in the Catholic missions can be more easily resolved than one might think. Preached in its essentials, Christian teaching is not all that hard to grasp. It is a world religion – 'universalist' – rather than a 'Spanish' or 'European' faith. The missionaries brought European culture and values with them, and this may have got in the way of their success. But it is a mistake to believe that Catholicism spread throughout the world in the Counter-Reformation era because it was advanced by imperialist forces. The native Japanese martyrdoms I mentioned showed that the missionaries in that country had produced a genuine appreciation of Christianity. Japanese appreciation had nothing to do with the factors of prestige and power. On the other hand, it of course helped enormously if the Christian faith could be presented in the languages of the peoples, even if its concepts might be new and strange. In Japan much trouble was taken by the missionaries to learn and transcribe the language. The missionaries with the greatest chance of success were those like Roberto di Nobili who preached in the style of a Hindu penitent; or Alexandre de Rhodes who quickly learned the native speech in Indo-China and took much of the credit for his claim of 300,000 baptisms in Tonking by 1649; or the Bishop Toribio de Mogrovejo, whose number of converts was mentioned above and who had learned the Indian language Quechua.

A complex formula has to be worked out between Christianization and acculturation, that is, the acceptance by missionaries of the culture of the people or the imposition by the missionaries of their cultures on resident peoples. This formula can be assembled not by historians but by theorists and practitioners of mission. Today, Christian missionaries emphasize assimilation to 'native' cultures. They try to recruit a native clergy and seek thereby to make themselves redundant as soon as possible.

Before we leave the subject of Counter-Reformation missions

beyond Europe four further points are worth making. First, the mission to the further world from the sixteenth century onwards had been prepared by the missionary work of the 'regular' orders, especially the preaching orders of Dominicans and Franciscans, in late medieval Europe. These 'popularizers of Christianity' developed the skills of explanation that were subsequently used in the extra-European missions. Second, as the missions abroad proceeded they were paralleled by missions in Europe. There were early missions of re-conversion such as the campaigns of the Jesuit Peter Canisius (1521–97) who covered 20,000 miles on foot and horseback in thirty years in the German and Czech lands. In the seventeenth century the regular 'missions to the countryside' were launched upon alleged 'pagan' or 'semi-pagan' areas of Europe, such as southern Italy, Britanny and Normandy. 'Catholic Europe in the Tridentine period', says Delumeau, 'hummed with travelling missioners.' The techniques they used were similar to those employed in the mission fields outside Europe. Third, a distinction should be made between the mission abroad to native peoples and the Christian care of Europeans outside Europe. The most successful example of the latter is the survival of Catholicism, despite many difficulties, in French Canada. There the descendants of peasants from Normandy increased their numbers at a phenomenal rate. 'They were', says Delumeau, 'a sturdy population immune to the "Enlightenment" of the eighteenth century', a people, too, who for a long time preserved the authentic atmosphere of seventeenth-century French Catholic piety. Fourth, it might be of interest to consider the Catholicization of the map, at least the map of Spanish America and the western United States. Spanish explorers and their chaplains sometimes gave names to places according to the feast of the day of their arrival at a site:

Los Angeles	California	(Our Lady of) the Angels
Sacramento	California	(The Blessed) Sacrament
Vera Cruz	Mexico	True Cross
Santa Fé	New Mexico	Holy Faith
San Francisco	California	Saint Francis
Rosario	Argentina	(The) Rosary
San Diego	California	Saint James

San Salvador	El Salvador	Holy Saviour
Concepcion	Chile	(The Immaculate) Conception (of Mary)
Corpus Christi	Texas	The Body of Christ
Trinidad	Caribbean	(The Holy) Trinity

Conclusion

Our survey of missions in the last section allowed us to see the furthest geographical extension of the Counter-Reformation. This widely accepted term presupposes, as we saw at the beginning of this pamphlet, that the Counter-Reformation was primarily a movement of opposition to the Protestant Reformation. As far as missions were concerned, such a motive hardly arose in Catholic minds: the 'Protestant threat' did not direct the thinking of Catholics in the mission field. The extent to which the Counter-Reformation was preoccupied with countering Protestantism depends on which aspect of the process we are considering and where we are seeing the phenomenon in operation. For instance, if we looked at the Counter-Reformation in Germany and the other 'border lands' between the two faiths, we should see a heavy concentration on combatting Protestantism; whereas, if we regarded Italy and Spain, once the relatively minor Protestant invasion of the sixteenth century had been repelled, the Catholic renewal in those countries was concerned mostly with raising levels of Catholic piety and instruction.

The Counter-Reformation cannot be separated from the political history of early modern Europe, and especially with the accentuation of the authority of national and territorial states. In the sixteenth and seventeenth centuries rulers tended to enhance their authority over the Church, whether Catholic or Protestant, within their states. This meant a further diminution of the legal authority of the pope over the international Catholic Church and over the states of Europe; the papacy may have consolidated its spiritual role over the Church, but it must have been too remote an institution to act as a charismatic focus for the mass of Catholic Europeans. The individual Catholic had his heroes and heroines, though; these were the saints. Some of them rose to a new prominence in the Counter-Reformation period. St Joseph, for instance, who had enjoyed scant regard in the middle ages, began to assume importance as the personification of a favourite Counter-Reformation virtue, chastity. Imbued by a scholarly and fastidious spirit, the Counter-Reformation looked closely at the credentials of saints and gave diminished importance to legendary or semi-legendary figures such as St George and St Christopher.

As to spurious practices of the middle ages, such as the commercialized indulgence that had aroused Martin Luther's ire, the Counter-Reformation Church firmly set its face against them. Such practices were mechanistic, that is to say they relied on a formal performance of rites and routines for the individual's sanctification and salvation. Emotive religion was far from unknown in the middle ages, but its importance increased enormously in the Counter-Reformation period. By this I mean that Catholics were now encouraged even more than in the past to *feel* their religion: when they attended confession, for instance, they were stimulated to undergo an emotional sorrow for their sins and even repentance for having caused the sufferings of Christ. In the Eucharist, the communicant was taught to feel a personal glow of gratitude to Christ as an individual visitant. More frequent use of these sacraments was expected of the devout, and an intense, almost mystical, emotional response to them was looked for. The baroque art forever associated with, indeed created by, the Counter-Reformation played an indispensable part in the fostering of a deeply felt Catholic piety.

So the Counter-Reformation was a religious movement that affected, and was affected by, the cultural and political history of early modern Europe. It played a major part in the Europeanization of the non-European world. For four hundred years the mentality of the Counter-Reformation held sway in Catholic Europe. The Council of Trent launched the process, the Second Vatican Council closed it.

Select bibliography

(Place of publication is London unless otherwise stated.)

This bibliography is divided into general background works and more specific works dealing with the Counter-Reformation in particular.

For the whole period covered by this pamphlet the *New Cambridge Modern History* series provides the most comprehensive general coverage:
Volume II, *The Reformation 1520–59*, ed. G. R. Elton (Cambridge University Press, 1958).
Volume III, *The Counter-Reformation and Price Revolution 1559–1610*, ed. R. B. Wernham (Cambridge University Press, 1968) is obviously the nearest volume to our subject.
Volume IV, *The Decline of Spain and the Thirty Years War 1609–48*, ed. J. P. Cooper (Cambridge University Press, 1970).
Volume V, *The Ascendancy of France 1648–88*, ed. F. L. Carsten (Cambridge University Press, 1961).

For the late medieval and modern periods of European history, there is A. G. Dickens, *The Age of Humanism and Reformation: Europe in the 14th, 15th and 16th Centuries* (Englewood Cliffs, NJ: Prentice-Hall, 1978).
An excellent textbook for the sixteenth century is A. G. Koenigsberger and G. L. Mosse, *Europe in the 16th Century* (Longmans, 1971).
The period of the Reformation is dealt with concisely and expertly by G. R. Elton, *Reformation Europe 1517–1559* (Fontana, 1969) and by A. G. Dickens, *Reformation and Society in Sixteenth-Century Europe* (Thames and Hudson, 1966).
The second half of the Reformation century is well covered by J. H. Elliott, *Europe divided 1559–1598* (Fontana, 1968).

More specifically on the Counter-Reformation see A. G. Dickens, *The Counter-Reformation* (Thames and Hudson, 1969).

Notably Catholic standpoints are presented in P. Janelle, *The Catholic Reformation* (Collier-Macmillan, 1971), H. Daniel-Rops, *The Catholic Reformation* (Dent, 1963) and *The Church in the Eighteenth Century* (Dent, 1964).

H. Jedin's work is difficult for many students but a compressed version of his work on the Counter-Reformation council is available in *Crisis and Closure of the Council of Trent* (Sheed and Ward, 1967).

M. O'Connel, *The Counter-Reformation* (New York: Harper & Row, 1974) is a highly readable survey and as I have indicated J. Delumeau, *Catholicism between Luther and Voltaire* (Burns and Oates, 1977) has revised all thinking about the Counter-Reformation.

Works on the Jesuits include: C. Hollis, *A History of the Jesuits* (Weidenfeld, 1968), J. Brodrick, *The Origin of the Jesuits* (Longmans, 1949) and J. Brodrick, *The Progress of the Jesuits* (Longmans, 1946).

Two examples of Counter-Reformation saints' lives are J. Brodrick, *Robert Bellarmine, Saint and Scholar* (Burns and Oates, 1961) and J. Brodrick, *Saint Peter Canisius* (Chapman, 1963).

For an account of someone who, from the Catholic point of view, was decidedly not a saint, Carlo Ginzburg's *The Cheese and the Worms* (Routledge & Kegan Paul 1982), the book already referred to in the text.

NOTES

NOTES

NOTES

NOTES

NOTES